MW01288560
this journal belongs to:
365 days of self-love
52 weeks of healing
12 months of discovery

WRITE YOUR FAVORITE THING ABOUT YOURSELF BELOW

WHAT GOAL DID YOU ACHIEVE TODAY?

• even the tiniest of goals matter, write at least one. •

DATE

DATE

DATE

DATE

DATE

DATE

DATE

WEEK
2

WHAT GOAL DID YOU ACHIEVE TODAY?

• even the tiniest of goals matter, write at least one. •

DATE

DATE

DATE

DATE

DATE

DATE

DATE

I WILL STITCH MYSELF
BACK TOGETHER AGAIN
WHEN I AM READY
IN THE MEANTIME.
I WILL HOLD MY OWN HAND
AND KEEP MY HEART STEADY.

WEEK
3

SOME THINGS THAT BRING ME JOY

▲

▲

▲

▲

▲

▲

▲

WHAT GOAL DID YOU ACHIEVE TODAY?

• even the tiniest of goals matter, write at least one. •

DATE

DATE

DATE

DATE

DATE

DATE

DATE

WEEK
4
YOU ARE ALLOWED TO FEEL EVERYTHING,
TO BREAK IT ALL DOWN PIECE BY PIECE.

HEALING

IS TAKING EACH PIECE
FOR WHAT THEY ARE,
AND CARRYING ON,
STEP BY STEP,
SCAR BY SCAR.

WHAT GOAL DID YOU ACHIEVE TODAY?

• even the tiniest of goals matter, write at least one. •

DATE

DATE

DATE

DATE

DATE

DATE

DATE

SELF CARE MAY BE...

- FORGIVING YOURSELF
- CRYING WHEN YOU NEED TO CRY
- FRESH AIR
- WRITING, DANCING, LAUGHING
- RESTING WHEN YOU NEED TO REST
- ACKNOWLEDGING WOUNDS TAKE TIME
- HAVING BOUNDARIES
-
-
-

SELF CARE MAY NOT BE...

-
-
-
-
-
-
-
-
-
-

WEEK 5

WHAT GOAL DID YOU ACHIEVE TODAY?

• even the tiniest of goals matter, write at least one. •

DATE

DATE

DATE

DATE

DATE

DATE

DATE

YOU ARE
DESERVING
OF ALL THE
INTRICATE
AND BEAUTIFUL
THINGS
THIS WORLD HAS
TO OFFER

.
.
.

WEEK 6

WHAT GOAL DID YOU ACHIEVE TODAY?

• even the tiniest of goals matter, write at least one. •

DATE

DATE

DATE

DATE

DATE

DATE

DATE

BUILD
YOURSELF
EVERY DAY,
GROW FROM
THE HURT,
EMBRACE
ALL THE LOVE
YOU ARE
WORTH

WEEK 7

WHAT GOAL DID YOU ACHIEVE TODAY?

• even the tiniest of goals matter, write at least one. •

DATE

DATE

DATE

DATE

DATE

DATE

DATE

WHAT MAKES YOU FEEL MOST LIKE YOU?

YOUR EXISTENCE IS VALID!

WHAT GOAL DID YOU ACHIEVE TODAY?

• even the tiniest of goals matter, write at least one. •

DATE

DATE

DATE

DATE

DATE

DATE

DATE

YOU SURVIVE BY ACKNOWLEDGING
WHAT CAUSED THE PAIN,
YOU SURVIVE BY REMINDING YOURSELF
YOU ARE ENOUGH,
OVER AND OVER AGAIN

WEEK 9

WHAT GOAL DID YOU ACHIEVE TODAY?

• even the tiniest of goals matter, write at least one. •

DATE

DATE

DATE

DATE

DATE

DATE

DATE

BEING VALUED IS FEELING IMPORTANT, APPRECIATED AND WANTED

LIST THE PEOPLE THAT MAKE YOU FEEL VALUED

TELL THEM THAT YOU LOVE THEM

WEEK 10

WHAT GOAL DID YOU ACHIEVE TODAY?

• even the tiniest of goals matter, write at least one. •

DATE

DATE

DATE

DATE

DATE

DATE

DATE

INSIDE THE CHAOS,

IT IS IMPORTANT TO VALUE

YOUR SELF WORTH.

REMEMBER, YOU ARE THE MOON,

THE SUN, THE OCEAN

BRINGING BEAUTY TO THE EARTH.

WEEK 11

WHAT GOAL DID YOU ACHIEVE TODAY?

• even the tiniest of goals matter, write at least one. •

DATE

DATE

DATE

DATE

DATE

DATE

DATE

MY DREAMS HAVE DRIPPED THROUGH SUNLIT GLASS
SOMETIMES BEYOND THE HORIZON
YET STILL SO BEAUTIFUL

WHAT IS YOUR BIGGEST DREAM?

WRITE IT DOWN, REMEMBER IT, SAVOUR IT, MAKE IT COME TRUE.

WHAT GOAL DID YOU ACHIEVE TODAY?

• even the tiniest of goals matter, write at least one. •

DATE

DATE

DATE

DATE

DATE

DATE

DATE

YOU CAN DO ALL THAT IS IN YOUR HEART, ALL THAT IS IN YOUR MIND, ALL THAT IS IN YOUR SOUL

WHAT ARE SOME THINGS YOU WOULD LIKE TO DO MORE OF?

▲

▲

▲

▲

▲

▲

▲

WEEK 13

WHAT GOAL DID YOU ACHIEVE TODAY?

• even the tiniest of goals matter, write at least one. •

DATE

DATE

DATE

DATE

DATE

DATE

DATE

WEEK 14

A WORK IN PROGRESS STILL HAS CHARACTERS THAT BREATHE, CHAPTERS THAT MATTER AND ADVENTURES THAT ARE IMPORTANT. YOU ARE STILL A MASTERPIECE EVEN IF YOU HAVE SPACE TO GROW.

WHAT GOAL DID YOU ACHIEVE TODAY?

• even the tiniest of goals matter, write at least one. •

DATE

DATE

DATE

DATE

DATE

DATE

DATE

WHAT MISTAKES HAVE YOU MADE AND HOW DID YOU LEARN FROM THEM?

(WRITE IN THE SPACE BELOW)

WEEK 15

WHAT GOAL DID YOU ACHIEVE TODAY?

• even the tiniest of goals matter, write at least one. •

DATE

DATE

DATE

DATE

DATE

DATE

DATE

WEEK 16

I LOVE THOSE MOMENTS, IN THE EARL
EST HOURS OF THE MORNING, LOOKIN
AT A SKY BLANKETED IN DUSTY STARS
HAVING A CONVERSATION THAT MEANS
MUCH MORE.

WHAT IS THE MOST IMPORTANT CONVE
SATION YOU'VE EVER HAD?

(WRITE ABOUT IT HERE)

WHAT GOAL DID YOU ACHIEVE TODAY?

• even the tiniest of goals matter, write at least one. •

DATE

DATE

DATE

DATE

DATE

DATE

DATE

WHAT KEEPS YOU AWAKE?

WHAT GOAL DID YOU ACHIEVE TODAY?

• even the tiniest of goals matter, write at least one. •

DATE

DATE

DATE

DATE

DATE

DATE

DATE

WEEK 18

WHAT ARE SOME THINGS CURRENTLY DRAINING YOUR ENERGY?

(FILL THE SPACE BELOW)

LET THEM GO

WHAT GOAL DID YOU ACHIEVE TODAY?

• even the tiniest of goals matter, write at least one. •

DATE

DATE

DATE

DATE

DATE

DATE

DATE

WEEK 19
WHAT PLACE
MAKES YOU FEEL
MOST ALIVE?

WHAT GOAL DID YOU ACHIEVE TODAY?

• even the tiniest of goals matter, write at least one. •

DATE

DATE

DATE

DATE

DATE

DATE

DATE

Worrying finds me like the sea finds the sand,
always in the quiet moments, always when I need
[illegible]

What do I worry about most?

Divide them into what you can control and what you can't

What I can control

What I can't control

WHAT GOAL DID YOU ACHIEVE TODAY?

• even the tiniest of goals matter, write at least one. •

DATE

DATE

DATE

DATE

DATE

DATE

DATE

WEEK 21

WHAT GOAL DID YOU ACHIEVE TODAY?

• even the tiniest of goals matter, write at least one. •

DATE

DATE

DATE

DATE

DATE

DATE

DATE

A LIST OF THINGS
THAT MAKE ME SMILE

WHAT GOAL DID YOU ACHIEVE TODAY?

• even the tiniest of goals matter, write at least one. •

DATE

DATE

DATE

DATE

DATE

DATE

DATE

YOU ARE A PRIORITY
YOU ARE THE LIGHT
YOU ARE ALLOWED TO DO
WHAT YOU NEED
WHAT FEELS RIGHT

WHAT GOAL DID YOU ACHIEVE TODAY?

• even the tiniest of goals matter, write at least one. •

DATE

DATE

DATE

DATE

DATE

DATE

DATE

WEEK 2

WHAT GOAL DID YOU ACHIEVE TODAY?

• even the tiniest of goals matter, write at least one. •

DATE

DATE

DATE

DATE

DATE

DATE

DATE

WEEK 25

WHAT ARE SOME OF YOUR CURRENT PRIORITIES?
SHARE SOME OF THEM BELOW.

WHAT GOAL DID YOU ACHIEVE TODAY?

• even the tiniest of goals matter, write at least one. •

DATE

DATE

DATE

DATE

DATE

DATE

DATE

What makes you special?

Use the space below to write about yourself

WHAT GOAL DID YOU ACHIEVE TODAY?

• even the tiniest of goals matter, write at least one. •

DATE

DATE

DATE

DATE

DATE

DATE

DATE

LISTEN TO YOUR
SOUL, WHEN THE
PATH FEELS DARK AND
UNKNOWN. TRUST
YOURSELF, TRUST
THAT EVERYTHING IS
GOING TO BE OKAY,
TRUST THAT YOU ARE
NEVER ALONE.

WEEK 27

WHAT GOAL DID YOU ACHIEVE TODAY?

• even the tiniest of goals matter, write at least one. •

DATE

DATE

DATE

DATE

DATE

DATE

DATE

WHAT IS A REFLECTION TO YOU?

WHAT GOAL DID YOU ACHIEVE TODAY?

• even the tiniest of goals matter, write at least one. •

DATE

DATE

DATE

DATE

DATE

DATE

DATE

WHAT MAKES YOU PROUD?

LIST SOME OF YOUR ACHIEVEMENTS

WEEK 29

WHAT GOAL DID YOU ACHIEVE TODAY?

• even the tiniest of goals matter, write at least one. •

DATE

DATE

DATE

DATE

DATE

DATE

DATE

WEEK 30

WHAT GOAL DID YOU ACHIEVE TODAY?

• even the tiniest of goals matter, write at least one. •

DATE

DATE

DATE

DATE

DATE

DATE

DATE

SOMETIMES YOUR HEART WILL ACHE, SOMETIMES YOU'LL FEEL LONELY. SOMETIMES YOUR SOUL WILL BEND AND BREAK. BUT HOME IS NEVER THAT FAR AWAY, COME HOME DARLING, YOU ARE NEEDED, PLEASE STAY.

WHAT GOAL DID YOU ACHIEVE TODAY?

• even the tiniest of goals matter, write at least one. •

DATE

DATE

DATE

DATE

DATE

DATE

DATE

IF I COULD
GO BACK IN TIME,
I WOULD TELL MYSELF...
WEEK 32

WHAT GOAL DID YOU ACHIEVE TODAY?

• even the tiniest of goals matter, write at least one. •

DATE

DATE

DATE

DATE

DATE

DATE

DATE

YOU ARE RESPONSIBLE FOR YOUR OWN HEALING, BUT
THAT DOESN'T MEAN YOU CAN'T ASK FOR HELP.

WHAT THINGS DO YOU WANT TO HEAL?

WEEK 33

WHAT GOAL DID YOU ACHIEVE TODAY?

• even the tiniest of goals matter, write at least one. •

DATE

DATE

DATE

DATE

DATE

DATE

DATE

WRITE A LOVE LETTER TO THE LEAST FAVORITE THING ABOUT YOURSELF...

WHAT GOAL DID YOU ACHIEVE TODAY?

• even the tiniest of goals matter, write at least one. •

DATE

DATE

DATE

DATE

DATE

DATE

DATE

WHAT MAKES YOU THE MOST CONFIDENT? LIST THEM BELOW

WEEK 35

WHAT GOAL DID YOU ACHIEVE TODAY?

• even the tiniest of goals matter, write at least one. •

DATE

DATE

DATE

DATE

DATE

DATE

DATE

WRITE SOME PHRASES
THAT YOU LIKE TO LIVE BY
IN THE SPACE ABOVE

WHAT GOAL DID YOU ACHIEVE TODAY?

• even the tiniest of goals matter, write at least one. •

DATE

DATE

DATE

DATE

DATE

DATE

DATE

YOU CAN HIDE FROM THE WORLD, DEEP UNDER BLANKETS OR IN A CAVE MADE ONLY FOR YOU. BUT SOONER OR LATER IT WILL BE TIME TO BREATHE THE SCENT OF POPPIES AND FRESHLY MOWED LAWN. TO HEAL WHAT HAS BEEN HURT AND ALL THE THINGS THAT ARE RIPPED AND TORN. SO FOR ALL THE REASONS LIFE BECAME HEAVY, AND THE ROAD ROUGH, JUST KNOW THAT TODAY, TOMORROW AND ALWAYS, YOU ARE ENOUGH.

WHAT GOAL DID YOU ACHIEVE TODAY?

• even the tiniest of goals matter, write at least one. •

DATE

DATE

DATE

DATE

DATE

DATE

DATE

WEEK 38

THERE IS SO MUCH OF ME,
I KEEP HIDDEN.
LIKE MAGIC STORED UNDER ROCKS,
AND STORIES LOST ON SHELVES.
MORE THAN ANYTHING,
I WISH EVERYONE IN THE WORLD,
COULD BE UNAPOLOGETICALLY
THEMSELVES.

WHAT GOAL DID YOU ACHIEVE TODAY?

• even the tiniest of goals matter, write at least one. •

DATE

DATE

DATE

DATE

DATE

DATE

DATE

WEEK 39

WHAT GOAL DID YOU ACHIEVE TODAY?

• even the tiniest of goals matter, write at least one. •

DATE

DATE

DATE

DATE

DATE

DATE

DATE

TWINKLING LIGHTS AND DAYDREAMS
ALWAYS TASTE SO SWEET
MY HEART OPEN TO THE WILD
GROWING MYSELF IN EVERY BEAT

WEEK 40

WHAT GOAL DID YOU ACHIEVE TODAY?

• even the tiniest of goals matter, write at least one. •

DATE

DATE

DATE

DATE

DATE

DATE

DATE

MY PERFECT DAY LOOKS LIKE

WEEK 41

WHAT GOAL DID YOU ACHIEVE TODAY?

• even the tiniest of goals matter, write at least one. •

DATE

DATE

DATE

DATE

DATE

DATE

DATE

THE HEALING IS MY OWN, COMPASSION TO THE LONG DAYS AHEAD, BRAVERY TO THE WINGS I WILL SPREAD

WHAT DOES HEALING MEAN TO YOU?

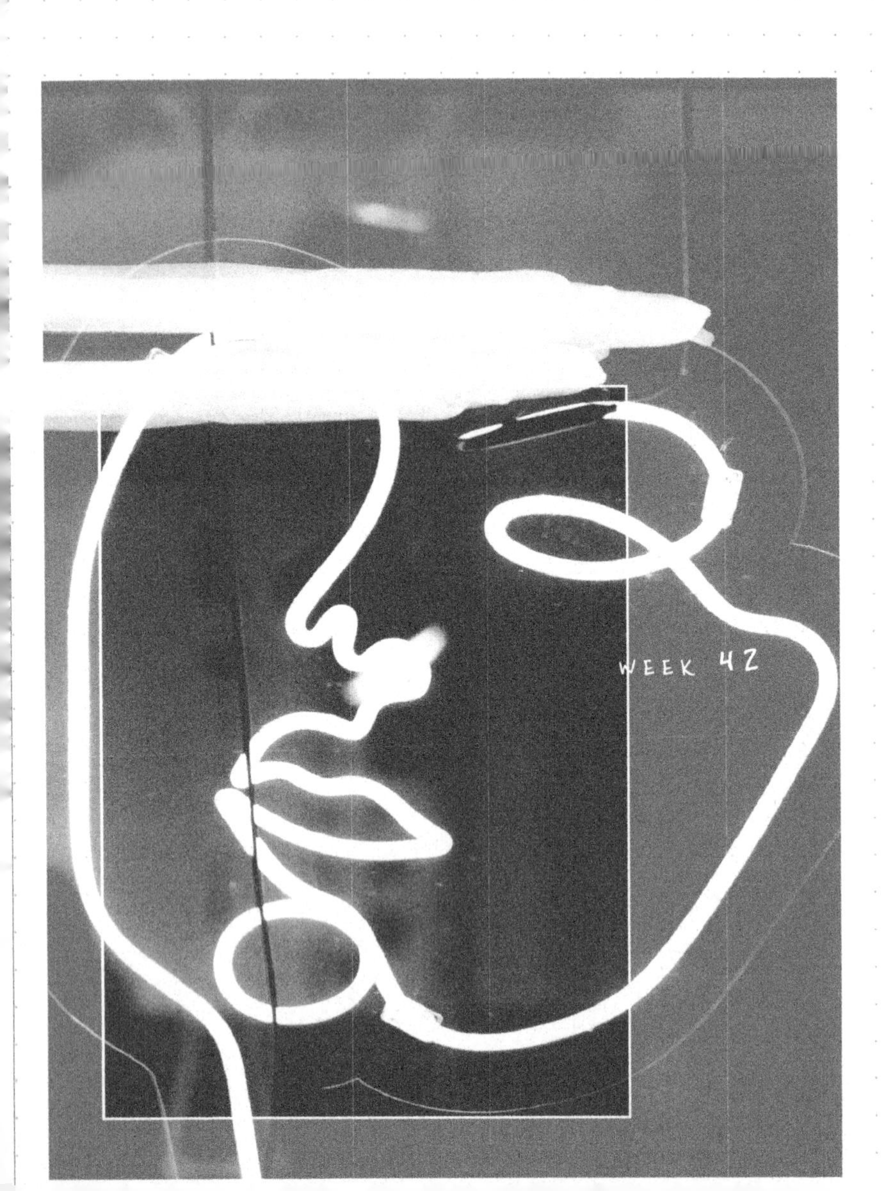

WHAT GOAL DID YOU ACHIEVE TODAY?

• even the tiniest of goals matter, write at least one. •

DATE

DATE

DATE

DATE

DATE

DATE

DATE

HOW CAN YOU BE KINDER TO YOURSELF?
LIST THEM BELOW

WEEK 43

WHAT GOAL DID YOU ACHIEVE TODAY?

• even the tiniest of goals matter, write at least one. •

DATE

DATE

DATE

DATE

DATE

DATE

DATE

MY SUPPORT CIRCLE

WEEK 44

WHAT GOAL DID YOU ACHIEVE TODAY?

• even the tiniest of goals matter, write at least one. •

DATE

DATE

DATE

DATE

DATE

DATE

DATE

WEEK 45

WHAT GOAL DID YOU ACHIEVE TODAY?

• even the tiniest of goals matter, write at least one. •

DATE

DATE

DATE

DATE

DATE

DATE

DATE

WHAT IS A QUOTE YOU LIVE BY?

WHAT GOAL DID YOU ACHIEVE TODAY?

• even the tiniest of goals matter, write at least one. •

DATE

DATE

DATE

DATE

DATE

DATE

DATE

THE CHAPTER WILL GO ON
DESPITE THE HEARTACHE OF THE ONE BEFORE.
YOU WILL READ ON, FORGE THROUGH,
RECAPTURE THE THINGS YOU LOVE,
ALL THE THINGS THAT MAKE YOU, YOU.

WEEK 47

WHAT GOAL DID YOU ACHIEVE TODAY?

• even the tiniest of goals matter, write at least one. •

DATE

DATE

DATE

DATE

DATE

DATE

DATE

It won't always be like this:
exhausting, soul crushing, stagnant.
You will rise, climb mountains,
paint the sky brilliant colors.
You are a vision, a miracle,
a wonder.

WHAT GOAL DID YOU ACHIEVE TODAY?

• even the tiniest of goals matter, write at least one. •

DATE

DATE

DATE

DATE

DATE

DATE

DATE

WHAT ARE SOME PLACES YOU GO TO THINK AND PROCESS YOUR THOUGHTS AND FEELINGS?

WHAT GOAL DID YOU ACHIEVE TODAY?

• even the tiniest of goals matter, write at least one. •

DATE

DATE

DATE

DATE

DATE

DATE

DATE

CHECK IN WITH YOURSELF

HOW AM I FEELING TODAY?

WHAT ISN'T WORKING?

WHAT IS WORKING?

DO I NEED TO BREATHE?

WHAT GOAL DID YOU ACHIEVE TODAY?

• even the tiniest of goals matter, write at least one. •

DATE

DATE

DATE

DATE

DATE

DATE

DATE

WEEK 51

FORGIVENESS IS THE SUN
RETURNING AFTER THE DARKEST DAY.

WHAT ARE THE THINGS YOU NEED TO
FORGIVE YOURSELF FOR?

WRITE BELOW

WHAT GOAL DID YOU ACHIEVE TODAY?

• even the tiniest of goals matter, write at least one. •

DATE

DATE

DATE

DATE

DATE

DATE

DATE

I AM THE GREATEST ADVENTURE

WRITE A LETTER TO YOUR FUTURE SELF.

WEEK 52

WHAT GOAL DID YOU ACHIEVE TODAY?

• even the tiniest of goals matter, write at least one. •

DATE

DATE

DATE

DATE

DATE

DATE

DATE

I love you.

Made in the USA
Coppell, TX
11 December 2020